SIR DAVID WILLC

A CELEBRATION
IN CAROLS

MUSIC DEPARTMENT

OXFORD
UNIVERSITY PRESS

OXFORD
UNIVERSITY PRESS

Great Clarendon Street, Oxford OX2 6DP,
United Kingdom

Oxford University Press is a department of the University of Oxford.
It furthers the University's objective of excellence in research, scholarship,
and education by publishing worldwide. Oxford is a registered trade mark of
Oxford University Press in the UK and in certain other countries

This collection © Oxford University Press 2014

Each composer has asserted his/her right under the Copyright, Designs
and Patents Act, 1988, to be identified as the Composer of their Work(s)

First published 2014

Impression: 2

All rights reserved. No part of this publication may be reproduced,
stored in a retrieval system, or transmitted, in any form or by any means,
without the prior permission in writing of Oxford University Press

Permission to perform the works in this anthology in public
(except in the course of divine worship) should normally be obtained
from a local performing right licensing organization, unless the owner
or the occupier of the premises being used already holds a licence
from such an organization. Likewise, permission to make and exploit a
recording of these works should be obtained from a local mechanical
copyright licensing organization

Enquiries concerning reproduction outside the scope of the above
should be directed to the Music Rights Department, Oxford University Press,
at music.permissions.uk@oup.com or at the address above

ISBN 978-0-19-340501-1

Music origination by Enigma Music Production Services, Amersham, Bucks.

Printed in Great Britain on acid-free paper by
Halstan & Co. Ltd, Amersham, Bucks.

FOREWORD

It was choir practice night in November 1961 at the church in London where my prodigiously gifted school friend John Tavener was organist and I was an occasional back-row choir member. He arrived brandishing a green book I had not seen before, sat down at the organ and immediately played the 'Sing, choirs of angels' verse from *O come, all ye faithful*. It was as if the night sky had suddenly lit up. Several of us clustered round the single copy of *Carols for Choirs* at the organ and sang David Willcocks's marvellous descant there and then, before excitedly turning the pages to explore some of his other newly-published carol arrangements in the book which was to transform the world's musical celebration of Christmas. If my fairy godmother had whispered to me that night 'there will be four more volumes of this amazing collection before the century is over, and you will co-edit them with David Willcocks', I would have laughed, but in the years which followed it came to pass.

David became a mentor, supporter, and friend to me, and it gives me untold pleasure to see fifteen of his classic carols gathered together in this new collection, plus three new carols composed in his honour by, respectively, his son Jonathan; his former King's College chorister and choral scholar Bob Chilcott; and myself. Happy 95th birthday, Sir David! You have made all our Christmases merry.

John Rutter

INDEX OF ORCHESTRATIONS AVAILABLE FOR HIRE/RENTAL

The following orchestral accompaniments are available to hire from the publisher's Hire/Rental Library or appropriate agent. Please quote the Hire Index number when ordering material.

Orchestrations are shown numerically to correspond with the traditional layout of an orchestral score, thus '2.1.2.1 – 4.3.3.1 – timp – hp (opt.) – str' indicates an orchestra comprising 2 flutes, 1 oboe, 2 clarinets, 1 bassoon; 4 horns, 3 trumpets, 3 trombones, tuba; timpani, harp (optional), and strings.

CAROL	SCORING	HIRE INDEX NO.
Away in a manger	strings	9
Birthday Carol	• 2.2.2.2 – 4.2.3.1 – perc – str	196
	• 2tpt, hn, tbn, tuba	281
	• 4tpt, 3tbn, tuba, 2perc (including timp)	11
Hark! the herald-angels sing	• 2.2.2.2 – 2.3(3opt.).3(opt.).1(opt.) – timp, perc – str	38
	• strings	38
	• 4tpt, 3tbn, tuba, perc, organ	200
Jingle, Bells	• 2.2.2.2 – 4(3&4opt.).3(3opt.).3.1 – timp, 2perc – org (opt.) – str	187
	• 4tpt, 3tbn, tuba, 2perc, organ	188
	• 2tpt, hn, tbn, tba, 3perc, pno (opt.)	198
O come, all ye faithful	• 2.2.2.2 – 2.3(3opt.).3(opt.).1(opt.) – timp, perc – str	62
	• strings	62
	• 3tpt, 3tbn, timp	27
	• 2tpts, 2hns, 2tbns, timp	27
	• 4tpt, 3tbn, tuba, perc, organ	200
Quelle est cette odeur agreable?	strings	79
Rejoice and sing!	2(picc).2.2.2 – 2.2.3.1 – timp, 2perc – hp – str	402
Resonemus laudibus	• 2picc.2.2.2 – 2.3.3.1 – timp, perc – pno (opt.) – str	85
	• 4tpt, 3tbn, tuba, timp, 2perc	129
Sussex Carol	• 2picc.2.2.0 – 0.0.0.0 – org/pno – str	104
	• strings	104

Away in a manger

Anon. 19th cent.

Melody by W. J. Kirkpatrick (1838–1921)
arr. DAVID WILLCOCKS

In verse 3 the whole choir may hum whilst a treble soloist sings the words.

© Oxford University Press 1960 and 2014. Photocopying this copyright material is ILLEGAL.

I saw three ships

Trad. English carol
arr. DAVID WILLCOCKS

Dynamics are left to the discretion of the conductor.

© Oxford University Press 1960 and 2014. Photocopying this copyright material is ILLEGAL.

8

O come, all ye faithful

Adeste, fideles

Trans. F. Oakeley,
W. T. Brooke,
and others

Words and melody by
J. F. Wade (1711/12–86)
arr. DAVID WILLCOCKS

Verses 1–5 may be sung by unison voices and organ, SATB voices and organ, or voices unaccompanied as desired.
Verses 3–5 may be omitted. The harmonies used for verses 1–5 are from *The English Hymnal*.

© Oxford University Press 1961 and 2014. Photocopying this copyright material is ILLEGAL.

3. See how the shepherds,
    Summoned to his cradle.
Leaving their flocks, draw nigh with lowly fear;
    We too will thither
    Bend our joyful footsteps:

    O come, etc.

4. Lo! star-led chieftains,
    Magi, Christ adoring,
Offer him incense, gold, and myrrh;
    We to the Christ Child
    Bring our hearts' oblations:

    O come, etc.

5. Child, for us sinners
    Poor and in the manger,
Fain we embrace thee, with awe and love;
    Who would not love thee,
    Loving us so dearly?

    O come, etc.

Glo - - - - - - - ry in the high - est:

Glo - ry to God in the high - est: O

O come, O come,

come, let us a - dore him, O come, let us a - dore him, O

let us a - dore him, Christ the Lord!

come, let us a - dore him, Christ the Lord!

ALL VOICES

Homage to R. V. W.

Sussex Carol

Trad. English carol
arr. DAVID WILLCOCKS

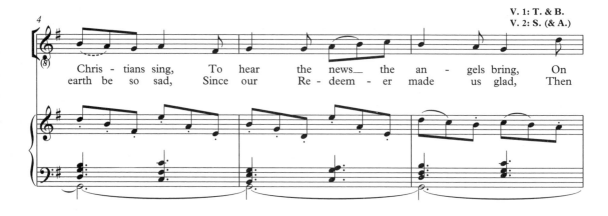

Melody and words reprinted by permission of Ursula Vaughan Williams.

© Oxford University Press 1961 and 2014. Photocopying this copyright material is ILLEGAL.

Infant holy, infant lowly

Trans. Edith M. Reed (1885–1933)

Polish carol
arr. DAVID WILLCOCKS

© Oxford University Press 1961 and 2014. Photocopying this copyright material is ILLEGAL.

Tomorrow shall be my dancing day

Trad. English carol
arr. DAVID WILLCOCKS

© Oxford University Press 1966 and 2014. Photocopying this copyright material is ILLEGAL.

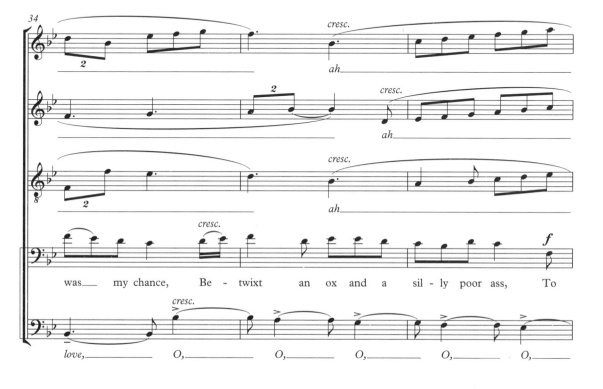

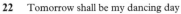

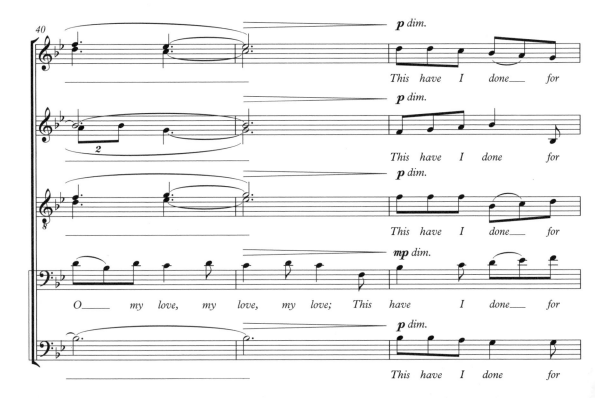

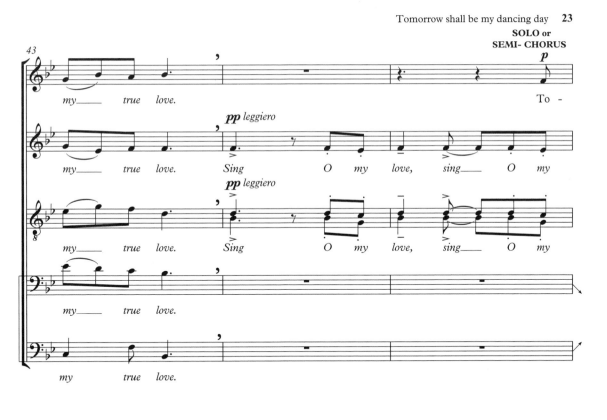

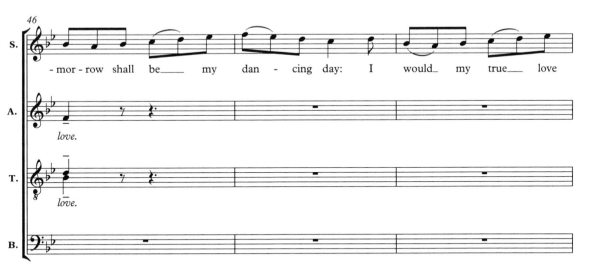

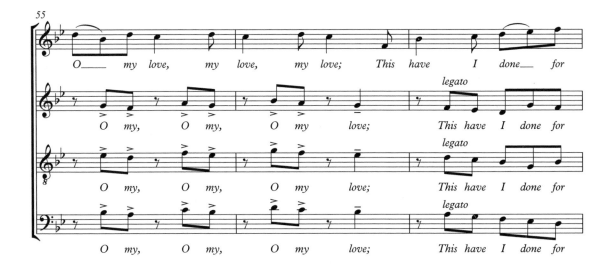

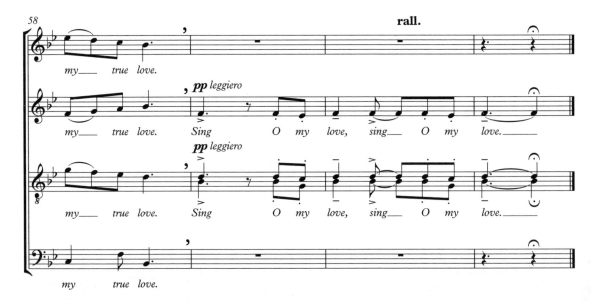

Hark! the herald-angels sing

Charles Wesley (1707–88)
and others

FELIX MENDELSSOHN (1809–47)*
v. 3 arr. DAVID WILLCOCKS

1. Hark! the he - rald - an - gels sing__ Glo - ry to the new-born King;
2. Christ, by high - est heav'n a - dored, Christ, the ev - er - last - ing Lord,

Peace on earth and mer - cy mild,__ God and sin - ners re - con - ciled:
Late in time be - hold him come__ Off - spring of a vir - gin's womb:

Joy - ful all ye na - tions rise,__ Join the tri - umph of the skies,__
Veiled in flesh the God - head see,__ Hail th'in - car - nate ¹De - i - ty!

With th'an - gel - ic host pro - claim, Christ is__ born in Beth - le - hem.
Pleased as man with man to dwell, Je - sus,__ our Em - ma - nu - el.

unis.

Verse 3 overleaf

Hark! the he - rald - an - gels sing Glo - ry__ to the new - born King.

Org.

Org. Ped.

*Melody, and harmony for vv. 1 and 2, adapted by W. H. Cummings (1831–1915) from a chorus by Mendelssohn.
Verses 1 and 2 may be sung by unison voices with organ if desired.

¹*Deity* pronounced *Dee-ity*

© Oxford University Press 1961 and 2014 (descant and organ part for verse 3). Photocopying this copyright material is ILLEGAL.

Quelle est cette odeur agréable?

Whence is that goodly fragrance flowing?

vv. 1–3 trans. A. B. Ramsay (1872–1955)
v. 4 trans. David Willcocks

Trad. French carol
arr. DAVID WILLCOCKS

English words of vv. 1–3 reprinted by permission of the Master and Fellows of Magdalene College, Cambridge.

© Oxford University Press 1970. Trans. for vv. 1–3 © Magdalene College, Cambridge. Used by permission.
Photocopying this copyright material is ILLEGAL.

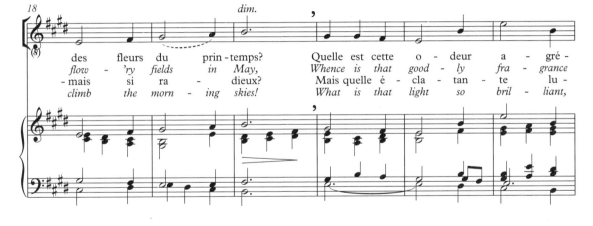

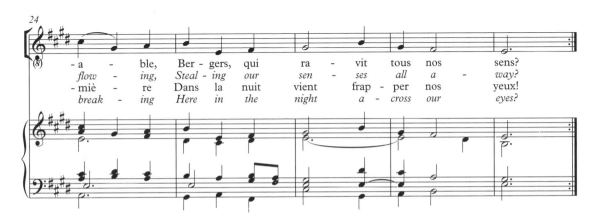

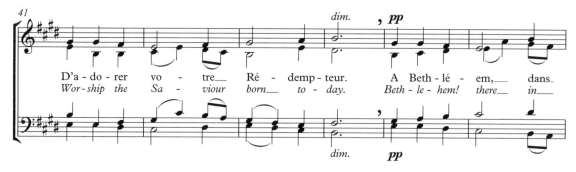

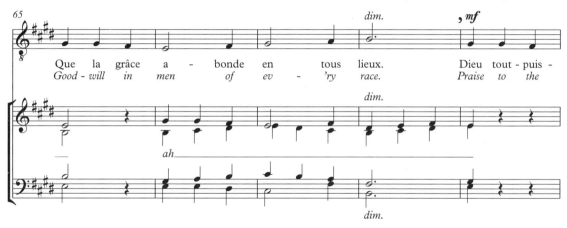

Que la grâce a - bonde en tous lieux. Dieu tout - puis -
Good - will in men of ev - 'ry race. Praise to the

ah

- sant, gloire é - ter - nel - le Vous soit ren - du - e
Lord of all cre - a - tion, Glo - ry to God the

ah   ah

ah   ah

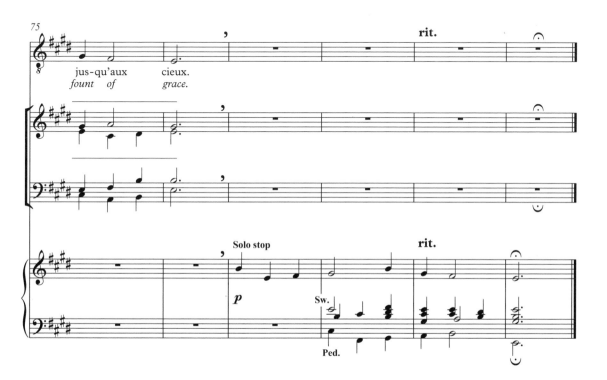

jus-qu'aux cieux.
fount of grace.

Gabriel's Message

S. Baring-Gould (1834–1924)

Basque carol
arr. DAVID WILLCOCKS

© Oxford University Press 1970 and 2014. Photocopying this copyright material is ILLEGAL.

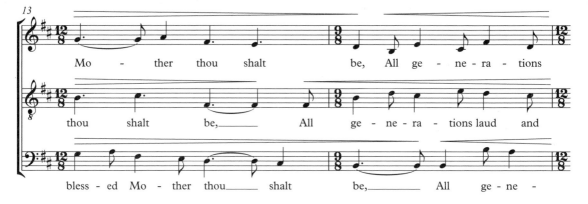

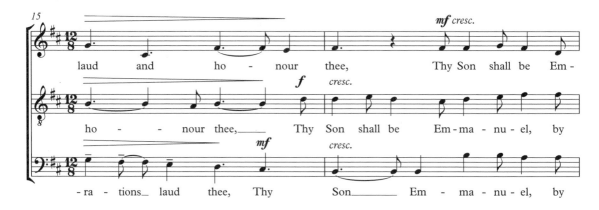

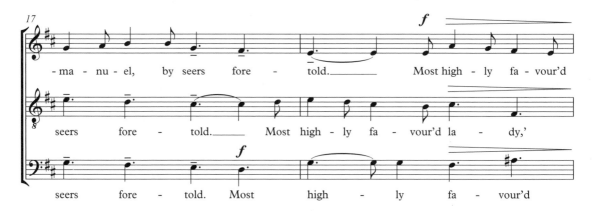

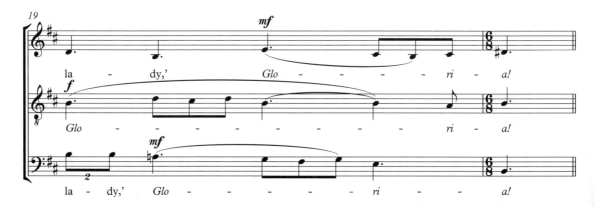

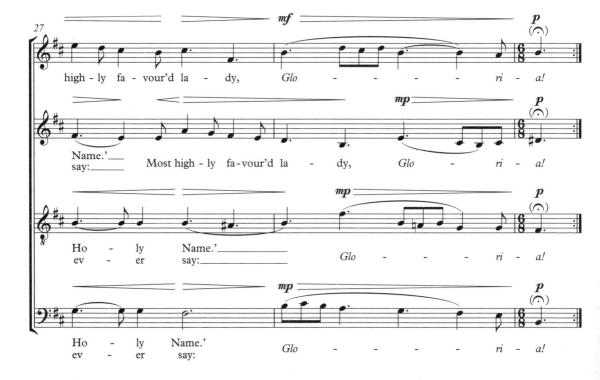

for The Bach Choir

Birthday Carol

*Words and music by
DAVID WILLCOCKS

*Words adapted from Luke 2
†Children and/or audience join in (optional)

© Oxford University Press 1974 and 2014. Photocopying this copyright material is ILLEGAL.

vv. 2, 4, and 6

SOPRANOS *legato*   *stacc.*

mf 2. Shep-herds a - bi - ding   in the field,   Al - le - lu -
f 4. 'Ti - dings of   joy to   you I   bring,'   Al - le - lu -
mf 6. A   host of   an - gels   fill'd the   sky,

ALTOS

legato   *stacc.*

mf

legato

To them God's   glo - ry   was re - veal'd.
- ia, 'To - day is   born a   heav'n-ly   King.'   Al - le - lu - ia.
Thus sing - ing   praise to   God on   high:

legato   *stacc.*

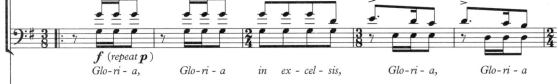

f (repeat *p*)   Glo - ri - a,   Glo - ri - a

S.
A.

Glo - ri - a,   Glo - ri - a   in ex - cel - sis,   Glo-ri - a,   Glo - ri - a

Glo - ri - a,   Glo - ri - a

T.
B.

f (repeat *p*)
Glo - ri - a,   Glo - ri - a   in ex - cel - sis,   Glo-ri - a,   Glo - ri - a

f (repeat *p*)

v. 7 (from previous page)   **ALL VOICES**   *ff*

7. Now join we all the an - gel -

\- throng, Al - le - lu - ia, And let our voi - ces swell the

song: Al - le - lu - ia, Glo - ri - a, Glo - ri - a

in ex - cel - sis, Glo - ri - a, Glo - ri - a

Resonemus laudibus

14th-cent. carol*
arr. DAVID WILLCOCKS

1. Re - so - ne - mus lau - di - bus___ cum jo - cun - di - ta - ti - bus___ ec - cle - si - am fi - de - li - bus. Ap - pa - ru - it___ quem ge - nu - it___ Ma -

*transcribed and edited by Frank Ll. Harrison

© Oxford University Press 1970 and 2014. Photocopying this copyright material is ILLEGAL.

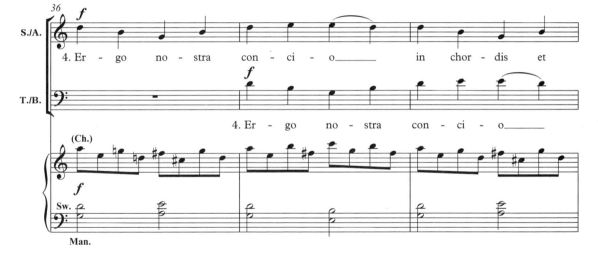

-ri - a.   5. Et De - o qui

-it__ Ma - ri - a.   5. Et De - o qui

(ALL VOICES)

ve - ni - as__ do - nat et lae - ti - ti - as__ nos e - i - dem

gra - ti - as. Ap - pa - ru - it__ quem

ge - nu - it__ Ma - ri - a.__

Jingle, Bells

Words and melody by
J. PIERPONT (1822–93)
arr. DAVID WILLCOCKS

© Oxford University Press 1987 and 2014. Photocopying this copyright material is ILLEGAL.

for John Rutter on his 60th birthday

Lullay, my liking

Anon. 15th cent.

DAVID WILLCOCKS

*Each verse may be sung by one or more upper-voice soloists, according to the resources of the choir.

© Oxford University Press 2006 and 2014. Photocopying this copyright material is ILLEGAL.

VERSE 2
SOLO *mp*

2. That e - ter - nal Lord___ is he___ that made al - le

D.C. Refrain

thing: Of al - le lord - es he is Lord, of al - le king - es King.

VERSE 3
SOLO *mp*

3. There was [1]mic - kle me - lo - dy at that Child - es birth: Al - though

D.C. Refrain

they were in hea - ven's bliss they ma - de mic - kle mirth.

VERSE 4
SOLO *mp*

4. An - gels bright they sang that night, and said - en to that Child:

D.C. Refrain

'Bless - ed be thou,___ and so be she___ that is both meek and mild!'

VERSE 5
SOLO *mp*

5. Pray we now to that Child and to his mo - ther dear,___ God

grant them all his bless - ing that now mak - en cheer!

Optional ending: after the refrain following verse 5, the soloists may sing their verses simultaneously, with a final refrain sung *pp*.

[1]mickle = much

Commissioned by Donald Stewart (KC 1941), in memory of his wife Beryl

High Word of God, eternal Light
Verbum supernum, prodiens

10th cent., trans. J. M. Neale
v. 5 adapted*

Sarum chant
arr. DAVID WILLCOCKS

*English translation from *The New Oxford Book of Carols*, edited by Hugh Keyte and Andrew Parrott.

© Oxford University Press 2008 and 2014. Photocopying this copyright material is ILLEGAL.

*If preferred, the organ may be saved until the final bar.

to Stephen Cleobury
and the Choir of King's College, Cambridge

Starry night

Anne Willcocks

DAVID WILLCOCKS

First performed on Christmas Eve, 2004, in King's College Chapel, Cambridge.

© Oxford University Press 2005 and 2014. Photocopying this copyright material is ILLEGAL.

BASS SOLO

Ho-ly maid in Beth - le-hem, strong and trust - ing, so se - rene,

Man.

An-gel voi - ces, soar-ing up-wards, greet the birth to this fair queen.

Ho-ly maid in

Beth - le-hem, al-le - lu - ia, strong and trust - ing, so se-rene, An-gel

Al-le - lu - ia, al-le - lu - ia, ve-lut ma - ris stel - la,___

33

voi- ces, soar-ing up-wards, greet the birth to this_ fair_ queen.

cresc.

mf Al-le-lu - ia, al-le-lu - ia, pa - rens et pu-el - la.

cresc.

f

37 **TENOR SOLO**

mf Shep-herds near to Beth - le-hem see the an - gels fill the_ sky,

cresc.

mp

cresc.

(Man.)

41 *f*

Hast - en now to - wards the won - der, find the king from heav'n on

mf

(*p*)

44

(*f*)

high. Al-le - lu - ia, al - le-lu - ia, O lux be-a - tis - si - ma,

S.
A.
mp *cresc.*

Shep-herds near to Beth - le-hem see the an - gels fill the sky,_____ Hast-en now to-

T.
B.
mp *cresc.*

49

Al - le - lu - ia, al - le-lu - ia, cor-dis in - ti - mis - si-ma.

mf

- wards the won-der, find the king_from heav'n on_ high.

mf

mf

Ho-ly child in Beth - le- hem, cra-dled in a man - ger_ poor,

Star a-bove pro-claims the sto - ry: source of hope for ev-er-more.

in celebration of the 95th birthday of Sir David Willcocks

Rejoice and sing!

Words by John Rutter,
incorporating a traditional carol text

JOHN RUTTER

* 7/8 bars in this carol always divide into 3 + 2 + 2

© Collegium Music Publications 2014. This edition exclusively licensed worldwide to Oxford University Press 2014.
All rights reserved. Photocopying this copyright material is ILLEGAL.

dawn - ing, For Christ is born in Beth - le - hem, On Christ - mas Day in the

morn - ing.

2. And   what was in those

T./B.

ships all three, On Christ - mas Day, on Christ - mas Day? And   what was in those

for David, with love and admiration

Nowell, nowell!

Trad. English
adapted from the Cornish Songbook

JONATHAN WILLCOCKS

© Oxford University Press 2014. Photocopying this copyright material is ILLEGAL.

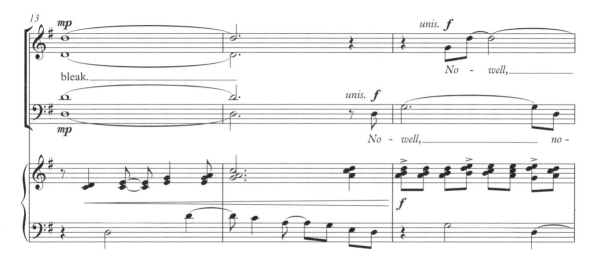

-el!

unis. *mf*

2. And then there did⏜ ap-
4. The star went forth⏜ un-

f

mf

S./A.

-pear⏜ a star⏜ In the East, its glo - ry did shine a - far.⏜ Un - to
-to the North West,⏜ Un - til o - ver Beth - le - hem did⏜ it rest.⏜ And⏜

earth⏜ it gave⏜ a great⏜ light, And⏜ there it con - tin -
there did re - main⏜ by night and by day,⏜ Right o - ver the place⏜

-ued day and night._____
____ where Je - sus lay._____

TENORS and BASSES

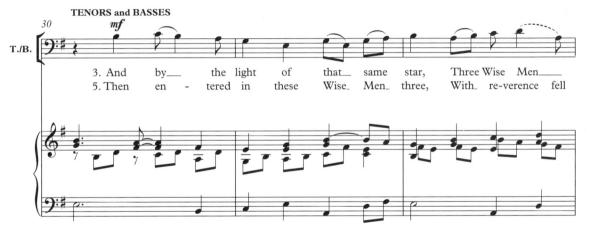

3. And by____ the light of that___ same star, Three Wise Men____
5. Then en - tered in these Wise_ Men_ three, With_ re-verence fell

came from far;____ To seek___ a King____ was their in - tent;____ They
on their knee.____ And of - fered there____ in His____ pre - sence The

fol-lowed the star_____ where - e'er it went._____
gifts_____ of gold_____ and frank - in - cense._____

S.
A.

unis. **f**

No - well,_____ no - well,__

T.
B.

unis. **f**

No - well,_____ no - well,

f

Born is the King of Is - ra - el!

6. Then

unis. **f**

mf

let us all with one ac-cord Sing prai-ses to our
unis. **f**
6. Then let us all with one ac-cord Sing prai-ses

hea-ven-ly Lord That hath made heav'n and earth of nought, And
to our Lord

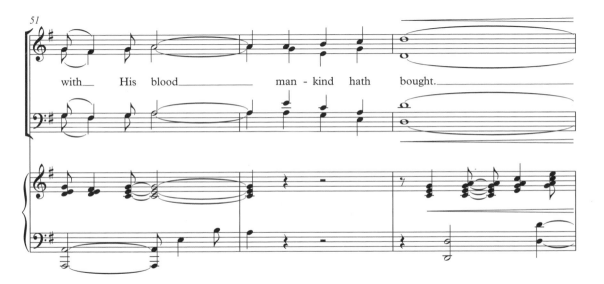

with His blood man-kind hath bought.

for Sir David Willcocks

There is no rose

Anon. 15th cent.

BOB CHILCOTT

© Oxford University Press 2014. Photocopying this copyright material is ILLEGAL.

¹A wonderful thing

² Of equal form

[3] Glory to God in the highest
[4] Let us rejoice

⁵ Let us follow

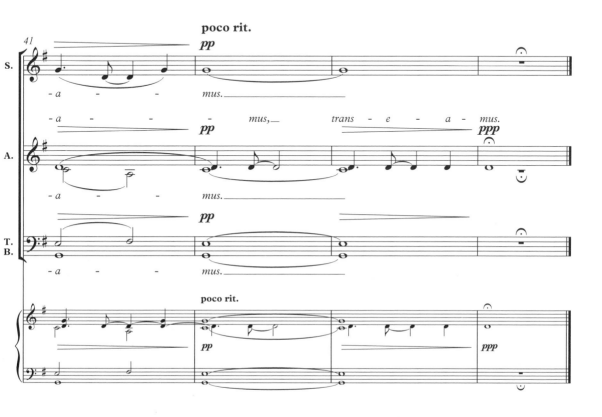